Brendan and The Whale

by Clare Maloney with illustrations by Jeanette Dunne

VERITAS

First published 2002 by

Veritas Publications

7/8 Lower Abbey Street

Dublin 1

Ireland

Email publications@veritas.ie

Website www.veritas.ie

ISBN 0 86217 645 X

A catalogue record for this book is available from the British Library.

Designed by Bill Bolger

Printed in the Republic of Ireland by Betaprint Ltd, Dublin

Veritas books are printed on paper made from the wood pulp of managed forests. For every tree felled, at least one tree is planted, thereby renewing natural resources.

In Clonfert one evening St Brendan sat listening
To St Berrind's tales from abroad
Of magnificent sea-creatures and marvellous birds
And the Land of the Promise of God.

So taken was Brendan by it all that, next morning
When the brothers assembled to pray
Brendan said, 'Brothers, I need your advice',
They listened to hear what he'd say.

'I am determined, brothers', he said
'Let it blow fair wind or ill
To set sail in search of the Land of Promise,
That's if – and only if – it's God's will'.

'What's your advice brothers, what do you say?'
They spoke with one voice, heart and mind
'You are our Abbot; your will is ours.
Where you go we follow behind.'

They built a boat – that looked not unlike
A banana – with black leather skin.
They gave it a mast, a sail and a blessing
And that was what they set sail in.

They sailed out west; sometimes the wind
Carried them swiftly along,
Sometimes it died down, so they rowed and they rowed
And battled many a storm.

They fasted their bodies and feasted their eyes
On the wonders of God at sea –
An Island completely covered in sheep
Big as cows and white as could be

A Paradise of Birds with the purest white feathers
Chanting psalms to the beat of their wings.
Brendan listened in amazement to one bird explaining
'We're what you might call "spiritlings"'

On another island a mysterious well
Whose water, though clear, ran deep
The more brothers drank, the deeper they sank
Into a deep, deep sleep.

Then a beast ploughed the sea, making waves so great
It seemed certain the boat would capsize,
Spouting foam from its nose, it bore down on the brothers
Who definitely now, feared for their lives.

But another monster, spitting fire and flames
Rose up suddenly, as if 'on cue',
Attacked and killed the first, then returned
Where it came from, out of the blue.

From The Island of Smiths a fierce, fiery people
Hurled huge burning rocks at the boat
These fell in the sea, which boiled up around them
And hissed and steamed and smoked.

But in North winds or South winds, in East winds or West,
Whatever their direction, God guided;
Through Advent, Christmas, Lent, Easter, Pentecost,
Whether hungry or thirsty, God provided.

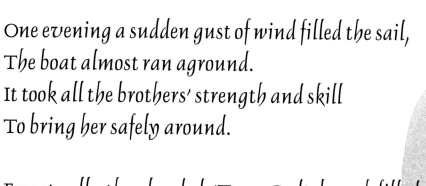

One evening a sudden gust of wind filled the sail,
The boat almost ran aground.
It took all the brothers' strength and skill
To bring her safely around.

Eventually they landed. 'Twas God's breath filled our sail',
'We are here', Brendan said, 'by God's grace'
But although he didn't say it to the brothers, he thought
'There's something fishy about this place'.

That day was Holy Saturday
A day of fasting and prayer
The brothers got out of the boat and knelt down
But Brendan kept vigil in there.

The day drifted quietly towards evening
Before silently fading from sight
In the empty boat on that island in the ocean
Brendan watched through the dead-of-night.

Stars broke out like beads of sweat
Glistening on night's blackened brow,
The wind held its breath like it dared not disturb
The saint's concentration now.

He cast his mind like a fishing line
With a hook on the end, ready-baited
Into the depths, while his body sat still
In the boat, and waited, and waited.

And still he sat motionless, his thoughts and his mind
Sinking down deeper and deeper
As though he might fathom something of God
In the nature of the sea and its creatures.

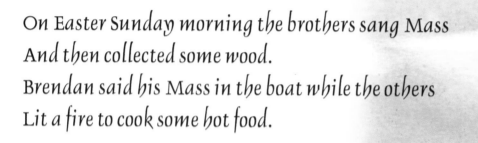

On Easter Sunday morning the brothers sang Mass
And then collected some wood.
Brendan said his Mass in the boat while the others
Lit a fire to cook some hot food.

They put some meat in a pot of water
Which they hung on the fire. Next thing
A shudder ran through the ground where they stood
And the island – yes, the island – was moving!

Abandoning everything the brothers rushed
To the boat in fear and dread.
Brendan reached out and drew each one on board
Whereupon they set sail and fled.

Taking one look behind them the brothers could see
At a distance of over two miles,
The island still moving, the fire still burning
They stared at it, shading their eyes.